A Teacher's Guide to Successful Classroom Management and Differentiated Instruction

Wrinkles in Teaching:
A Series of Guidebooks for Teachers

Wrinkle is "a useful piece of information," and one dictionary illustrates by saying, "Learning the wrinkles from someone more experienced saves time." In the case of teaching, it also promotes faster, more effective student learning; it prevents unnecessary and frustrating bouts of trial and error; and it results in greater satisfaction with the work. The "someone more experienced" is Billie Birnie, who taught successfully in elementary, middle, and senior high schools and then went on to observe and teach hundreds of teachers and, eventually, to write about her observations and experiences. Her books, designed for both elementary and secondary teachers, are short, practical, and down-to earth conversations about the craft of teaching. *A Teacher's Guide to Successful Classroom Management and Differentiated Instruction* was the first in the series.

It was followed by two books on organizational strategies, assessing writing, and (by Susan Maynard) parenting and learning disabilities. Readers are welcome to suggest additional topics for the series. Suggestions should be sent to Rowman and Littlefield.

A Teacher's Guide to Successful Classroom Management and Differentiated Instruction

Second Edition

Billie F. Birnie

ROWMAN & LITTLEFIELD
Lanham • Boulder • New York • London

Published by Rowman & Littlefield
A wholly owned subsidiary of The Rowman & Littlefield Publishing Group, Inc.
4501 Forbes Boulevard, Suite 200, Lanham, Maryland 20706
www.rowman.com

Unit A, Whitacre Mews, 26-34 Stannary Street, London SE11 4AB

British Library Cataloguing in Publication Information Available

Library of Congress Cataloging-in-Publication Data

Names: Birnie, Billie F., author.
Title: A teacher's guide to successful classroom management and differentiated instruction / Billie F. Birnie.
Description: 2nd edition. | Lanham, Md. : Rowman & Littlefield Education, 2017. | Includes bibliographical references.
Identifiers: LCCN 2016058836 (print) | LCCN 2016059840 (ebook) | ISBN 9781475833010 (cloth : alk. paper) | ISBN 9781475833027 (electronic)
Subjects: LCSH: Classroom management. | Individualized instruction. | Mixed ability grouping in education.
Classification: LCC LB3013 .B542 2017 (print) | LCC LB3013 (ebook) | DDC 371.102/4--dc23
LC record available at https://lccn.loc.gov/2016058836

∞ ™ The paper used in this publication meets the minimum requirements of American National Standard for Information Sciences Permanence of Paper for Printed Library Materials, ANSI/NISO Z39.48-1992.

Printed in the United States of America

Contents

Preface   vii

A Note About Names   xi

Acknowledgments   xiii

1 Using a Reflective Log   1

2 Classroom Management   7

　　The Basic Premise   8

　　Step 1: Know What You Want (and What You Don't
　　　　Want)   9

　　Step 2: Show and Tell Your Students What You Want
　　　　(and What You Don't Want)   13

　　Step 3: When You Get What You Want, Praise It—
　　　　Generously and Specifically   21

　　Step 4: When You Get Something Else, Act —Quickly
　　　　and Appropriately   25

　　In Closing   27

　　Resources   28

　　Notes   30

3 Differentiated Instruction   31

　　Differentiated Instruction: What It Is   32

To What Extent Do You Already Differentiate
    Instruction?   34
What It Looks Like   37
Before You Start   42
How to Do It   43
If You're Apprehensive   48
Resources   48
A Word About High-Stakes Testing   50
Note   51

References   53

About the Author   55

Preface

Classroom management and differentiated instruction continue to emerge as two of teachers' greatest challenges, and while an abundance of books offer advice, systems, techniques, and examples, teachers still ask for a practical, down-to-earth, short guide to help them create the learning environment they want and to accommodate all of their students' needs.

I, too, understand those needs well, having faced them myself. My challenges with classroom management emerged, not when I was a rank amateur, but as an experienced teacher with a history of success. I taught both high school and elementary school in perfect bliss; then I moved to an urban middle school, totally unprepared for dealing with recalcitrant, unruly youngsters who almost drove me out of teaching. Had it not been for assistant principals Mary Lou Dunn and Michael Flynn, I might have joined the ranks of "leavers." Mary Lou dried my tears and told me I could succeed, and Mike came into my classroom day after day to teach me how. With their support I made it through that year.

Building on what they taught me, I continued to thrive for many years in teaching, first at that middle school and then in two large urban high schools. Eventually, experience and observation led me to formulate and master the steps described in this guide. They have been shared with hundreds of other teachers, who have used them successfully in their own classrooms—in elementary, middle, and senior high, in public, private, and parochial schools.

Differentiating instruction came more easily. It was apparent from the beginning that students varied greatly in their skills, interests, and learning styles, and that, if I were to be successful, I would have to plan instruction accordingly. I was fortunate that my first teaching assignment was high school journalism and the sponsorship of the school's newspaper and yearbook—roles that demand differentiation because of the necessity of individual assignments.

Transferring the concept to classes of language arts and social studies was a challenge, since those subjects are often taught through a whole-group approach, but I tackled the work with enthusiasm. And the payoff was worth the effort. As I told my students at the beginning of each term, "The only students who fail this course will be those who don't come to class or who don't complete assignments." And that was true: everyone who attended and did their work passed, and many of them excelled. I still hear from former students who appreciated the opportunity to march to their own drummers while meeting course requirements.

I can't dry your tears, and I can't come into your classroom to show you how to manage it and differentiate instruction, but I can share what I have learned in the hope that it will keep you in the profession and make your time in the classroom successful and satisfying.

A final word before we begin. In her stellar book *Mindset: The New Psychology of Success, How We Can Learn to Fulfill Our Potential*, Carol Dweck discusses the difference between a *fixed mindset* and a *growth mindset*. A person who has a fixed mindset believes that "your qualities are carved in stone" (p. 6); that is, that one's intellect and character are unchangeable. A person with a growth mindset knows that those basic qualities "are things you can cultivate through your efforts" (p. 7). Dweck goes on to say, "Although people may differ in every which way—in their initial talents and aptitudes, interests, or temperaments—everyone can change and grow through application and experience" (p. 7). That belief underlies everything in this book.

A Note About Names

The names of teachers who discussed the use of reflective logs are used with permission, as are their comments. All of the classroom examples are based on actual classroom experiences: some are composites, some are reports about teachers with whom I am no longer in contact, and some are descriptions of my personal experiences. For those examples, I have used pseudonyms. In addition, all student names are fictitious.

Acknowledgments

I am grateful to the following people, all of whom played essential roles in the creation of this book:

- Sister Suzanne Cooke, formerly headmistress of Carrollton School of the Sacred Heart and now head of the Conference of Sacred Heart Schools, for her encouragement to write the book on differentiated instruction and for her support of its first publication.
- Susan Maynard, PhD, for her enthusiasm for the development of ideas that extended her own thinking, expressed in *The Low-Down on Learning Disabilities*.
- Former assistant principals Mary Lou Dunn, Michael Flynn, Andy Donelli, and Dr. Fred Rodgers, and guidance counselor Fred Burnside, all of whom supported me in my quest for control of the classroom.
- The many teachers who allowed me to observe them as they created healthy, happy, and effective learning environments. Those whose teaching is reflected in this book are Steve Alvers, Judy Willig Blanchard, the late Dr. Karen Dreyfuss, Fran Ginsberg, Marjorie Hull, Donald Jones, Jenny Oren Krugman, Lyn Larsen, Barbara Lima, Jackie McGee, Dr. Alicia Moreyra, James

Murray, Pete Murray, Margo Poulson, Barbara Quinaz, Mary Seamans, Steve Serrotte, Jane Simmons, Perry Slater, Charma Smith, Diane Victoria, Jenny Vogel Brain, and Sue White.

- Colleagues who participated in the online discussion on using reflective logs: Ms. Quinaz, Larry Plank, Shana Tirado, Sallie Snyder, Ayesha Hui, Theresa Graves, Tina Pipp, and Jill Germain.
- Dr. Eveleen Lorton, professor emerita at the University of Miami, Coral Gables, Florida; the late Sister Margaret Seitz, who was assistant headmistress at Carrollton School of the Sacred Heart; and my husband, Richard Birnie, for their careful review and cogent suggestions for both the first and second editions.
- Vice president and editorial director Tom Koerner, associate editor Carlie Wall, and production editor Chris Basso of Rowman & Littlefield for their invaluable editorial assistance in the publishing of this second edition.

Chapter One

Using a Reflective Log

Whether you want to refine your classroom management, learn to differentiate instruction, or improve some other aspect of your teaching, you'll find that using a reflective log, or journal, will facilitate your efforts. A well-kept log accomplishes three purposes: it records what happened in your classroom, it provides the opportunity to analyze what happened, and it reminds you of actions that will improve your craft.

A log may be as informal as random notes on your lesson plans or cell phone, or it may be as formal as a daily journal in a specialized format. The essential thing is that you write about your reflections in order to preserve them.

Terrie Graves, a science resource teacher at Robles Elementary School in Tampa, Florida, was trained to keep a log when she attended Marshall University in Huntington, West Virginia. She said, "I continued because I am a very reflective person and I find that it helps me keep track of my thinking." Terrie makes daily entries in her log "if I am finding things I need to work on," or, if nothing is pressing, at the end of a unit or a lesson. She cites as benefits of keeping a log the improvement of delivery of concepts and the ability to analyze students' learning— "tracking something about a student that doesn't make sense until I see the pattern."

Although she transfers notes and pictures to the log itself, Terrie's approach to recording first thoughts is eclectic: "I write notes in my cell phone, napkins, take pictures, notes in lesson plans and on the calendar. Making sure that I keep track of my 'wonderings.' I have tried the formal books, but my brain is more of a free spirit. It is what works for me."

Barbara Quinaz, lead teacher in the Cambridge Program at MAST Academy in Miami, Florida, has kept a reflective log throughout her twenty-seven years of teaching. Entries are made "daily, weekly, or biweekly, depending on how I'm feeling and my need to debrief." Asked about the benefits of keeping a log, she offered this response:

> I think the benefits of keeping a log are many. It helps me to sort out my ideas. I'm a very creative teacher, so when an idea comes to me or one of those "teaching moments," I must have a place to write them down and plan them out. A lesson plan for me is like a recipe card, but the teaching log and my responses are like the preplanning invitation, dinner conversation, and the after-party debriefing when the guests go home.

A teaching log is a reflection of my thinking. Sometimes, things outside of my classroom, out of my control, can interfere with my morale and taint my enthusiasm and positive teaching spirit. The teaching log grounds me and reminds me why I wanted to teach in the first place. It helps to fuel my ideas and sustain their implementation.

In addition, the teaching log helps me to capture those special teaching moments and stories that I want to remember always. When I eventually reread what I've written, it has the potential to bring me another dose of happiness and a smile to my face.

Like Terrie, though, Barbara feels comfortable with a variety of "data collection techniques." She reported, "My teaching log isn't always a narrative with complete sentences. I sometimes find myself writing out calendars and making lists, but I give myself permission to add those things. I think they make me feel more in control. I feel it's all a part of my creative teaching process."

Other teachers echoed those two, vouching for the advantages of keeping a log, attesting to the need for recording what happened in the classroom, and using the log as a reminder of what to do next time—whether the issue was addressing student behavior, teaching *Hamlet* again, designing an experiment, or making adjustments in methods of assessment. Some teachers, such as Tina Pipp at Bellamy Elementary School, code their lesson plans with symbols such as *G* for *Good* and *E* for *Excellent*, to remind themselves what really worked.

Others, such as Sallie Snyder, write notes to themselves: "Don't ever do this again!" or "Try this next time . . . " with a note on how to revise the lesson. "My notes were always helpful in reflecting on what worked and what didn't," Sallie said, "in changing my teaching methods, in responding to issues raised in class to address the next day or in the weeks to come."

Schoolteachers are not the only people who attest to the benefit from such reflections. Internationally known master woodworker Paul Sellers, also a teacher, wrote in his blog of June 29, 2016,

> Drawing and writing encapsulate much of the essence of what I felt at the time, and immediately I open a page in my journal I am transported right back to the very moment or moments of creativity I was engulfed in. Nothing, no other media, including film, can do this for me. The funny thing is that I may well have forgotten that I ever did this or that, so, for me, journaling is something I will always recommend.

A newcomer to keeping a reflective teaching log, librarian Jennifer Jarson, in her blog of September 4, 2015, summarized the literature on various methods of keeping a reflective log and recorded her personal goals for the activity. Five of those goals are applicable to any teacher:

- Document what I'm doing and learning so that it's less transitory.
- Direct and heighten my attention to what I care about in the classroom, what works and doesn't, and what helps students.
- Facilitate my thoughts on how to teach better.
- Capture evidence of student learning in individual classes and across classes.
- Generally try to connect some dots.

For his journal, Paul Sellers uses a sketch book with no lines, some writers prefer gridded paper, and others like an old-fashioned spiral-bound composition book. Still others use their computers. The format of the log itself should be something that appeals to you and invites you to write in it. If you've never kept a log before, you might want to try this simple three-column format.

Head the first column "What Happened," the second "What I Think About What Happened," and the third "What to Do." At the end of the teaching day in a place uninterrupted by distractions, write in the first column a reminder of the situation; it might include a date, the kind of class, or other identifying information. Then record an incident worthy of reflection. Just the facts—no editorializing. In the second column, jot down your reflections about the incident: why you chose it for the log, what led up to it, how you felt about it, what implications it had for your teaching— any critical or analytical reflections you wish to make. In the third column, write what you intend to do in the future as a result of the incident.

Two examples follow, the first a negative incident involving behavior in a third-grade math class and the second a positive incident dealing with methodology in a high school English class.

Both teachers in the examples decided for themselves what they needed to do as a result of the incidents they described. However, that may not always be the case. Sometimes, the action to take

Table 1.1.

What Happened	What I Think About What Happened	What to Do
March 23, 2016. Math. Sarah and Jeremy got into an argument about how to solve a word problem; they disrupted the whole class with their shouting, and they hurled insults at one another in the process. I lost my temper at both of them and by the time I had them subdued, a pall hung over the whole class.	S & J don't know how to express a difference in opinion without being confrontational. (Probably some of the other kids don't, either.) Ironically, both of their processes would have arrived at the right answer to the problem. I didn't behave well; I should never have lost my temper. The atmosphere of the whole classroom suffered as a result of the encounter. It's my responsibility to see that this kind of incident doesn't get out of hand. What can all of us learn from the incident?	Talk to the whole class tomorrow about "civil discourse" and its role in our culture. Frame the disagreement that S & J had about the problem, including both ways to solve it. Put the students in pairs and ask them to prepare a role-play in which S & J resolve the issue amicably. Over the next few days, let the students read their scripts. After we've heard all of them, talk about which ones were best and why. Second, remember what I learned about not reacting emotionally to children's negative behavior!
What Happened	What I Think About What Happened	What to Do
May 24, 2016. Fifth-period English. Today the students shared their pictures! To end the unit on *Macbeth*, I told the students that their "final exam" was to represent the play visually, with a drawing or painting (realistic or abstract) on a piece of typing paper. Each student had to show the picture and explain why the visual representation captured the essence of the play. Both the pictures and the explanations were fantastic!	All of us gained more insight into the play than I had thought possible. Some of the students who struggled with the traditional assessments excelled in this exercise. Their performance raised their self-esteem and also the regard of their peers. All of the students, even those who expressed reluctance about the assignment, enjoyed the activity.	Do it again! Write a note to Cedric's parents about how well he did on this assignment. He needs the encouragement. Work more art into all of the units. This is a largely untapped avenue to understanding in academic classes. Take the pictures to our next "show and tell" department meeting.

might be to consult with a colleague or mentor, to glean ideas from someone you trust about the best course of action.

Making the time in your days to keep a reflective log may well prove to be the greatest challenge. However, as with any good habit that improves the quality of your life (think eating well, exercising, balancing work and play, nurturing friendships), this one will more than repay you for the time it takes. It will help you to become the teacher you want to be.

Chapter Two

Classroom Management

Who can use this book? Any teacher who wants to improve the tenor of the classroom. Whether you teach in a school where student behavior is a constant challenge or in one where peace and harmony prevail, this book will help you create and sustain the learning climate you want. Whether you are a newcomer to the profession who needs to know how to establish order in your first year of teaching, a successful veteran looking for ways to fine-tune your classroom atmosphere, or someone in between looking for answers to questions about managing your classes, the steps offered here will help you achieve your goal.

Where does classroom management fit in? Successful classroom management goes hand in hand with effective teaching; in fact, the better the instruction, the less need there is for "managing" student attitudes and behavior, for they are shaped by enthusiastic engagement in learning. Classroom management might be considered the bread of a sandwich and instruction the filling; you need both framework and substance to make a sandwich or a successful classroom experience. This section focuses on the bread; if you want help with the filling, try the recipes in the second part of the book, on differentiated instruction.

How should this book be used? The plan here involves four steps; they are sequential and interdependent, and they are based on the premise explained below. Read the whole section through, taking time to do the exercises that are suggested. Then refine Step 1, implement Step 2, and take Steps 3 and 4 continually and consistently. Doing so will make your classroom a place where both you and your students want to be, a place where teaching and learning can be pursued without distractions.

THE BASIC PREMISE

Before learning the steps, consider the basic premise in which they are grounded. Underlying every successful classroom encounter is a positive relationship between teacher and students. Intentionally creating, nurturing, and sustaining those relationships are foremost among a teacher's responsibilities.

The relationship between teacher and students is a partnership—an unequal partnership, to be sure, for the teacher determines the tenor, sets the limits, and manages the interactions. The tenor may be formal, as it was in Paul Master's middle school history classes. Paul's erect carriage and booming voice reflected his military experience, and his love for both history and children imbued his lectures with enthusiasm and generosity. Students sat up straight, raised their hands for permission before speaking, and took notes to study for homework.

In contrast, the atmosphere may be informal and creative, as in Marlo Parsons's high school English classes, where the study of period literature was embellished with appropriate lighting, costumes, and a great deal of laughter. (Marlo frequently advised beginning teachers, "Remember that the students are not the enemy.")

Or the tone may be loving, as in Sofia Mora's fifth-grade class, where children thrived in a familylike atmosphere of shared responsibility and a continual celebration of learning.

Whatever the character of the partnership, to be successful, it must be grounded in trust. Trust is established when teachers back up words with actions, when they respond consistently from one day to the next, and when they keep their promises. Those are the teachers who employ the steps discussed here, and they are the teachers whose partnerships flourish.

For some teachers in some circumstances, a positive relationship emerges naturally. That may be the situation in which you find yourself. The pitfall in those cases is that teachers may be seduced into thinking that they have to do nothing to create or nurture the partnership. They may, understandably, take it for granted. On the other hand, a teacher may be faced with children who are angry, tired, or unruly. The relationship gets off to a bad start and deteriorates with every passing day, forcing the teacher to react continually to disruptive behavior.

While the positive experience is clearly more desirable than the negative, both may be no more than happenstance—and happenstance is not a firm foundation for a classroom partnership. The best teachers leave nothing to chance. They employ the four steps that follow to establish and maintain the relationship they desire.

STEP 1: KNOW WHAT YOU WANT (AND WHAT YOU DON'T WANT)

Good teachers know to begin planning for instruction by considering results first: What do they want students to know and be able to do at the end of the teaching and learning cycle? Strange as it may seem, however, many teachers never ask that question in terms of students' behavior and attitudes. Too many teachers take whatever comes as it comes, and as a result, some days are good, some are mediocre, and some are horrible. Not knowing why, such teachers muddle through, day after day, reacting to instead of shaping their environment.

This is no way to run a classroom, even for those fortunate enough to teach in a peaceful school where children are courteous and considerate. The learning climate of the classroom is the responsibility of the teacher, just as surely as the instructional approach is, and it behooves teachers to think about what kind of climate they want before ever setting foot in the classroom.

Consider a negative example that illustrates the point. Bob Britton met his tenth-grade science class on the day before a big football game, with his department head observing. After he presented the lesson, Bob made an assignment that students were to complete independently. As they began working, Bob walked up and down the rows of desks, looking over students' shoulders. He stopped next to a football player and asked, "So, Jay, are you ready for the big game?" Jay responded in the affirmative, and within minutes, half a dozen of the students were engaged in the conversation about the game, and the whole class was listening to it.

Then Bob called for silence and told the students to return to their assignments. It took a few minutes for them to regain their concentration, but they did as they were told—until Bob stopped at another student's desk and started another conversation about the game. This cycle repeated itself four times before the bell rang, and each time it took Bob longer to restore silence. The assignment was never completed.

When Bob met later in the day to review the class with his department head, they talked about what had happened. It didn't take Bob long to figure out that he was distracting students rather than supporting them in their work. The problem lay in his failure to determine beforehand what he wanted—and didn't want. As a consequence, his students, who were trying hard to follow his lead, vacillated between trying to work and trying to talk about the upcoming game.

So where do you begin? By visualizing the ideal classroom for you and your students. Do you envision an orderly, purposeful setting in which groups of students are working together on projects? Do you see some students working independently at learning centers while others do seatwork or read from the classroom library? Do you imagine students sitting attentively and listening as you explain a concept or demonstrate a skill? Perhaps your students are working in a laboratory or a studio, on a playing field, or in a gymnasium.

Exercise: Visualize the ideal lesson. Choose a lesson that you have taught successfully, or, if you have no experience yet, one that you are confident about teaching. Close your eyes. "See" the entire lesson in your mind, including as many details as you can. Use these questions to guide your visualization exercise: What does the room look like? What are you wearing? How are you feeling—about the lesson, the students, yourself? What resources will you and the students use during the lesson? How many students are involved? How many boys? Girls? What is their general demeanor? (Remember, this is an ideal lesson, so see them with the attitudes and behaviors you want!)

How do you greet the students? Open the class? What do you do to secure their attention and to "set the stage" for the lesson? Have they done homework? If so, how will you handle it? Do you need to distribute materials? Form groups? Do a demonstration? Present a lecture? Conduct a discussion? How will you manage transitions from one part of the lesson to another?

Go through the whole lesson, "seeing" exactly what you do, what the students do, and what the results are. Take the class all the way through to dismissal, and envision saying goodbye to the students before you open your eyes.

If it helps you to think through the details, do the exercise in writing.

Exercise: Make lists of "What I Want" and "What I Don't Want."[1] Drawing on the visualization of the ideal lesson, make two lists on one sheet of paper. On the left-hand side of the paper, list all of the things you want in your classroom. On the right-hand side, list the things you don't want. Think in terms of student attitudes and behavior.

For instance, under "What I Want," you might list words and phrases such as *respect, courtesy, love, purposefulness, laughter, good study habits, Standard English, effective presentation skills, all assignments completed on time,* and so forth. (Aim high, and remember what Goethe said: "If you treat an individual as he is, he will remain how he is. But if you treat him as if he were what he ought to be and could be, he will become what he ought to be and could be." Today's students are eminently capable of exemplary behavior and positive attitudes; as teachers, we need to expect the best of them.)

Under "What I Don't Want," you might include words and phrases such as *swearing, hitting, inattentiveness, alienation, rudeness, passivity, eating and drinking, grooming, tardiness, unexcused absences, late or incomplete assignments, sleeping, bad attitudes,* and so forth. Make the lists as detailed as you can. The clearer you are about what you want and don't want, the more likely you are to have the classroom of your dreams.

Exercise: Identify actions that demonstrate the most desirable and most undesirable conditions. Using the lists from the last exercise, choose the most important conditions (both those you want and those you don't want) and describe, in writing, teacher and student behaviors that manifest those characteristics. For example, when Jaquintha Sims did this activity, respect was at the top of her list. She recognized that, if respect is present in a classroom, everyone listens attentively when anyone is speaking, students and teacher know each other's names and use them, and both teacher and students employ common courtesies such as saying "please" and "thank you." (For a full discussion of respectful behavior and how to attain it, see "Promoting Civil Discourse in the Classroom" in the April–June edition of the Kappa Delta Pi *Record*.)

Among the conditions Jaquintha least wanted was passivity. She knew that passivity is evident when students refuse to participate in class discussions, when they put their heads on their desks, or when they attend to something other than the lesson.

The more specific you are in describing the behaviors you want and don't want, the better prepared you will be to implement the next step.

STEP 2: SHOW AND TELL YOUR STUDENTS WHAT YOU WANT (AND WHAT YOU DON'T WANT)

If you know what you want but your students don't, you may still end up with chaos in the classroom. The next step to successful classroom management is therefore to show and tell your students what you want and don't want. You show them by your own behavior and by calling attention to theirs, and you tell them, with both words and body language.

Janie White faced her advanced tenth-grade English class about a week after school had started. Janie had opened the class by announcing that she was going to return the first essays students had written, but before doing so, she was going to make some comments that would help all of them do better on the next assignment. The students were eager to receive their papers, and they sat attentively. Janie paused, leaned over the podium, and said, "If I were a student in an advanced tenth-grade English class and my teacher told me she was going to tell me something that would help me write better essays, I'd be scrambling for my pencil and paper so I could write down every word she said."

She paused again, and as she stepped back from the podium, thirty-six students scrambled for their pencils and paper so they could write down every word she said. When they were ready to write, Janie began her critique of their essays. She had told them what she expected, and they readily complied.

Oneitha Range teaches second grade in a school not far from Janie's. She spends a fair amount of time in the first week of school teaching her students how to enter the classroom, how to sit in their chairs, how to put their chairs under the tables before leaving the classroom, how to line up for lunch or dismissal, how to walk in the hallways ("head up, elbows in, no talking"), and how to use "twelve-inch voices" when they are working in groups. ("Your voice must be loud enough for a person twelve inches away to hear you, but soft enough that someone thirteen inches away can't hear you.") When children are working in groups, sometimes she carries a twelve-inch ruler around and holds it over the groups, to remind them of the desired noise level.

Fay Gaines, another English teacher, knows that her middle school students will be doing a great deal of peer editing in her class. At the beginning of each term, she assigns students to triads based on writing skill (one high, one medium, one low) and teaches them how to move into groups of three as quickly and quietly as possible, directing the rehearsal of movement from large group to triads and back again with a stopwatch in her hand.

Well into the semester, Fay announced time for peer editing. Students gathered their materials and moved into their groups in only twenty-six seconds. They could never have done it without clear directions and practice.

Sarah Billings wants students to use each other's names in class. In order for that to happen, she has to ensure that they know each other's names. On the first day of each school year, she introduces "The Name Game" by reminding students of "The Store Game" most of them played as children. In "The Store Game," the first child might say, "I went to the store and bought bananas." The second may add, "I went to the store and bought bananas and milk." The third: "I went to the store and bought bananas and milk and apples." And so forth.

Except with "The Name Game," students use only their first names. Told to look at each student as his or her name is spoken and not to write anything down, students recite their classmates' names, always in the same order, and adding their own to the end of the list. After playing for a few minutes, the tenth student would be expected to say, "Mary, John, Delores, Shanika, Abner, Carolina, Jose, Mercedes, Gerald—and I'm Terrence."

After everyone has been named, including the teacher, who must play as well, Sarah skips around, going back to students who had early turns. In about thirty minutes, forty students can hear, and many of them will learn, everyone's name in the class. A daily review during the first week and reminders to students to call each other by name fixes both the expectation and the knowledge for civil conversations. An added benefit for the teacher is that he or she, too, soon knows everyone's name, increasing students' feelings of belonging and removing the anonymity that can be a shield for misbehavior.

Another technique invaluable in setting expectations is the use of a letter to students, delivered and read to them on the first day of class. The one that follows comes from Julie Ryder, a high school English teacher. She explains that it will be a rare occasion for her to put printed material into their hands and then read it to them; she trusts their ability to read and comprehend for themselves. She explains further, though, that the content of the letter is so important to the success of the time they are about to spend together that she wants them to hear it from her. She also wants them to have the opportunity to ask questions, comment, or discuss the responsibilities that the letter describes. With that introduction, she distributes the letter and reads it to her students.

Dear Students:

Welcome to (name of class)! I look forward to working with you and to getting to know you during our time together. As we begin the new term together, let's review our responsibilities so the expectations for both of us will be clear from the outset.

As your teacher, I have the following responsibilities:

1. I must know the subject that I teach. I must stay abreast of current research in the field and continually strive to learn more about what I am teaching.
2. I must also continue to learn more about how to teach so that you will be able to learn more efficiently and more effectively.
3. I must be here every day that I can, and in case I have to be absent, I must provide plans that will enable you to continue learning in my absence.
4. I must plan all of our work so that you can master the objectives set forth by this course of study, whether they are prescribed by the national guidelines (name of national standards, if applicable), the state's (name of state's curricular guidelines), the district's (name of the district's guidelines), or a combination of these. That planning must encompass a wide breadth of material, with sufficient depth, and with attention to all of your learning styles and past experience—and it must be done for 180 school days, taking into account the many interruptions we will face.
5. I must implement those plans while staying attuned to a myriad of external forces that affect them—balancing, modifying, and clarifying where necessary. [Julie stops here briefly to be sure the students know what *myriad* means—their first vocabulary lesson of the year.] I must also make the instruction as relevant as possible, without giving in to the temptation of becoming an entertainer rather than a teacher.
6. I must monitor your progress and evaluate your performance in ways that promote your desire to succeed in class, being judicious and gentle but never dishonest in my assessment.

7. I must convey to you how much I enjoy being here, how I value the role I play in your life, and how I welcome the opportunity we have to learn together.
8. Finally, I must help you to discover the joy of learning—help you to realize that even though you might have originally come to this class because of external forces, you will eventually come of your own free will—because by fulfilling your responsibilities, enumerated below, you will learn not only the subject matter we pursue together but also something of value about yourself.

As my student, you have the following responsibilities:

1. You must come to class every day you are able. You must be in your seat prepared to work when the tardy bell rings, and you must not prepare to leave until I have indicated that you may do so. If you have to miss class, you must find out what you missed.
2. You must bring the necessary materials to class every day: your notebook, extra paper for taking notes, unlined paper for compositions, your writing guide, a pen, a pencil, your textbook, and electronic devices when appropriate. Your notebook should be ready for me to collect and evaluate at any time.
3. While you are in class, you must give your undivided attention to the work at hand. I will make every effort to provide activities that challenge your thinking and engage your attention. You must also do your part. If you feel sick, ask for a pass to the clinic. If you feel bored, feign attention [opportunity for another vocabulary lesson]; it will come with discipline. If you are distracted by external forces, remove yourself from them or discipline yourself to ignore them.
4. When you are confused (please note that I said "when," not "if"; if you are never confused, the course is too easy for you

and you should be seeking a different level of instruction)—
ask questions; and don't feign understanding if the answers
you receive are not clear. Continue asking questions until you
find what you seek. Also, don't assume that I know the answers to all of your questions. Sometimes a classmate, a
friend, a parent, another teacher, or a librarian will be able to
explain a concept more clearly than I can. Don't hesitate to
ask them for help.

5. Follow instructions and complete all assignments, both in and
out of class. The instructions and assignments that you receive are carefully considered; they are essential to the
smooth operation of the class and to your mastery of the skills
and concepts of the course. If you have concerns about your
instructions or assignments, discuss them with me; you will
find me receptive to your ideas, but do not take it upon yourself to ignore directions.

6. Study for this class regularly, even if you have no specific
assignment to complete. Review your notes, read your text,
find related materials in the library and online, think about
your work in progress. Much of what you learn will come
from regular, disciplined study.

7. NEVER, NEVER, NEVER CHEAT. You may be able to get
a higher grade by cheating; you may be able to fool me and
your parents and perhaps your classmates; but you will never
be able to fill the gap in learning caused by dishonesty and
shoddy scholarship. NEVER CHEAT.

8. Finally, when you are asked to evaluate the course of study,
the class activities, and my instruction, do so with the same
commitment that I bring to the evaluation of your performance. Your assessment of the class and of my teaching will
improve both, not only for you but also for those who follow
you.

I look forward to your year together. Let us welcome the challenges before us and face them with enthusiasm and commitment.

Sincerely, Julie Ryder, Your Teacher.

This message was obviously written for senior high school students and framed by Julie's personal standards and expectations. If you teach the same age of students and the letter says what *you* want it to say, by all means, use it. If it doesn't suit your philosophy or your writing style, you will want to modify it or write your own. Sam Smith, a fine high school social studies teacher, gave essentially the same message to his students on one page. His "contract" consisted of two columns, one that enumerated his responsibilities and one that stated those of his students.

Sarah Simons, a highly regarded teacher of upper-level mathematics, delivered a masterful letter to her students that concentrated primarily on a description of the kind of students who enrolled in her classes. (Of course, the students may or may not have been that kind of student when they arrived in her class; but the very fact that she acted "as if" instead of "wouldn't it be nice if" helped to begin forming the habits of mind and behavior she desired.)

Whatever approach you take, if you choose to use a letter, you will be most successful with it if you couch your message in positive rather than negative terms. Notice that Julie's letter includes only one admonition, or "don't"—the very strong one about cheating. The rest of the responsibilities are cast in positive terms.

Also, it makes good sense to let your students know what you expect of yourself as well as what you expect of them. If you seek a true partnership in learning, the roles of both teacher and students need to be clear.

Maria Ramos teaches elementary school; she uses, not a letter, but the following verse, which she and her students recite together at the beginning of each day. It embodies a philosophy for learning that encompasses both teacher and students:

We're a class with *heart*!
H is for *homework*, ready each day,
E is for *effort*, our best all the way.
A is for *asking*, as knowledge we seek,
R is for *raising our hands* when we speak.
T is for *thinking*, and that's what we do,
As we learn and we love and we laugh the day through.

And how do you show and tell our students what you don't want? One way is to ask students to demonstrate the undesirable behaviors and attitudes. Middle school students, for instance, especially enjoy demonstrating an unacceptable sound level. Before you ask them to do so, though, be sure they know the cue to bring the level back to normal. You might also ask students to demonstrate unacceptable posture, inattentiveness, off-task behavior, or mumbled speech. Such "staged" demonstrations are fun for students, and they offer the opportunity to use negative examples without putting any child on the spot.

Although Step 2 is most evident at the beginning of the school year, the best of teachers continue to show and tell their students what they want and don't want whenever the opportunity arises.

Exercise: List four things you might do to show students how to act or how not to act in your class. For instance, if you want students to be on time to class, you must always be there when they arrive. If you don't want them to eat or drink in the classroom, you must also refrain from doing so.

Exercise: Write four things you might say to tell students how to act or how not to act in your class. For instance, if you want students to say *please* and *thank you* and to use each other's names, you must set the example: "Larry, would you please collect the books and put them on the shelf?"

Exercise: Write an opening-of-school letter to your students, or adapt the one above for your use.

STEP 3: WHEN YOU GET WHAT YOU WANT, PRAISE IT—GENEROUSLY AND SPECIFICALLY

Having made sure that your students know what you want and don't want in the classroom, you are likely to have plenty of opportunities to implement Step 3. Remember the whole step, though, or your praise will not be as effective as it ought to be. Just saying, "Great!" "Wonderful!" or "Excellent!" in response to Joey's behavior may make everyone feel good, but it doesn't help the rest of the students know exactly what caused the sun to shine on Joe. "Great, Joey! You answered every one of your homework questions and turned them in on time!" gives both Joey and the rest of the class ample information to know what kind of behavior will produce that praise.

Complimenting students directly for desirable behaviors and attitudes goes a long way toward securing the classroom climate you want. For praise to have an even stronger effect, though, it should also be directed to others who are significant in the lives of your students. Blake Moore kept a stack of notepaper on his desk. When a student did something particularly praiseworthy, he would ask the student to stay after class for a moment while Blake wrote a quick note detailing the action.

Sometimes the note was to the student's parents, sometimes to a coach, band director, club sponsor, counselor, or administrator; the recipient was always someone who cared about the progress of the student. These notes not only rewarded students for good behavior or performance; they also strengthened the network of support that is so important for students' success. (If you're in a laptop school, you may want to use email instead of paper, although a handwritten note is more powerful than an electronic message.)

Following are examples of notes—the first to parents of a girl who frequently failed to do her homework, the second to the coach of a boy who was often tardy:

Dear Mr. and Mrs. Jones,

Josephine turned in her homework on time today, and she made an A on it.

I'm delighted, and I know you must be proud of her.

Sincerely,

Brenda Comer

English Teacher

Dear Coach Hanson,

John has been on time to my class every day this week, and his behavior has improved significantly. He even volunteered to collect homework today! I'm pleased with his progress and know you will be, too.

Sincerely,

Henry Carson

History Teacher

There will be times when a group of students, perhaps even an entire class, deserves your praise. Be generous with it; it costs you nothing, and it reinforces your expectations. "I love the orderliness of Table 4. Sasha, Jody, Ana, and Jose have done a splendid job of organizing their materials." "Thank you for your attentiveness; I can see that all of you are listening carefully to the instructions." "This class has surpassed my expectations for performance on the unit test! We had not one failure, and most of the grades are As and Bs!"

Like many teaching skills, praising effectively takes intention and practice. Develop your "vocabulary of praise" by doing the following exercises.

Exercise: Write a statement you could make to an individual student (for the whole class to hear) that praises him or her, specif-

ically and generously, for something he or she has done. For example, "Bethany, thank you for straightening the bookshelf without being asked. That was a valuable contribution to our learning environment."

Exercise: Write a note of praise to the parents of a student who has demonstrated one of your top three values. For example, if one of your top values is active engagement, the note might say, "Dear Mr. and Mrs. Avery, you will be pleased to know that Jonathan contributed to our class discussion on civic responsibilities. I am delighted with his effort. Sincerely, Mary Johnson."

Exercise: Write a statement that you could put on display that would praise one of your classes (the whole group) for demonstrating desirable conduct or achievement. Example: "Congratulations to third period! Class attendance has been 100 percent for five days in a row!"

Exercise: Develop or sketch a bulletin board or wall display that praises individual students. For example, a bulletin board filled with large stars on which exemplary student work is posted, with the caption, "This Week's Star Papers."

A Word About Rewards Other Than Praise. Some discipline plans offer specific rewards (e.g., points, candy, field trips) for good behavior. However, sincere praise, the pleasure of contributing to a positive classroom atmosphere, and increased joy in learning are rewards enough for good behavior. A classroom should be a place in which learning is valued for its intrinsic worth, not a place where children come to compete for pieces of hard candy.

That Being Said, Beware of the Pitfalls. Scott Aranha, a mathematics teacher and popular football coach, taught his assistant principal a valuable lesson. After watching him teach a challenging concept to his Algebra II students, the assistant principal asked Scott why he never praised his students. He had a ready answer. "When I was in high school, I played football for a coach who was always telling us how great we were, even when we weren't. We hated it because we knew the praise was insincere. I swore when I became a coach and teacher that I would never give false praise. I'd rather say nothing at all than to tell a student he's doing well when he isn't." Scott was right; students know immediately when praise is insincere or undeserved.

Another pitfall is to give in to the temptation to praise a student's innate ability rather than specific effort. Students need to be taught that success, in academics as in the rest of life, is something to be gained by effort. Telling children they are smart or talented or bright can lead to unrealistic expectations that are dashed by confrontation with work that is not easily accomplished. When faced with failure, children who have received such praise often give up, thinking they are not as smart as they had been led to believe. On the other hand, children who receive praise for their effort grow up knowing that learning can be challenging and that success comes, not because of innate talent, but because of hard work. [2]

But what does praise for effort sound like? Here are some examples:

- "I know this is difficult and I appreciate your effort."
- "This lesson (intonation, problem, etc.) is especially challenging; it requires lots of practice to get it just right."
- "My grandmother used to say that nothing easy is worthwhile; she would have thought this assignment worthy indeed. Keep trying and it will fall into place."
- "This passage (problem, dialogue, etc.) is really hard. It takes persistence to master it."
- "I can see from the quality of the characters (writing, diagram, homework, etc.) that you really put a lot of effort into this. That's admirable."
- "I like the fact that you didn't give up after the first try."
- "They say out West that when a bronco bucks you off, you should get right back on and ride him. The same is true with

these challenging problems. When one 'throws' you, go back to it and try again."

- "You've made several strong attempts here, and your performance (diction, characters, organization, etc.) is improving."

STEP 4: WHEN YOU GET SOMETHING ELSE, ACT — QUICKLY AND APPROPRIATELY

These guidelines are for the times when you get "something else."

If the misbehavior is minor and not violent: Gently redirect the student's behavior, as if you were channeling a stream. Annie Wharton demonstrated a masterful example of such rechanneling when she reviewed her class for a unit test. A student on the first row was looking at a large picture book instead of listening to the review. Annie stopped by his desk briefly, said, "That's a pretty book; why don't you look at it later?" Then she closed the book and continued the review.

A few minutes later, the boy opened the book again. Without missing a beat, Annie stepped to his desk, picked up the book, and placed it on her desk, all the time continuing the review. At that point, the boy had no option but to pay attention. And here's the beautiful touch of the master teacher: a few minutes before the end of class, Annie ended the review, picked up the book, and said to the class, "Joaquin brought this beautiful book from the library. Would you tell us what it's about, Joaquin?" Annie's control and insight had enabled her to seize the opportunity to validate a child's interest instead of overreacting to his initial inattentiveness.

If the behavior recurs, take the student aside and speak to him or her. Be sure the inappropriate behavior is specified so that the student knows exactly what you want corrected, and be sure that appropriate behavior is reinforced. For instance: "Mary, remember that we expect everyone to contribute positively to the lesson. Your remark about the lesson, even though it was whispered, detracts from our work. You must not make negative remarks about the assignments. If you feel that way about them, you may speak to me after class, and you know I will listen. But while we're working, if you can't say something nice, don't say anything at all." If possible, get a commitment from the student for a change in behavior.

If the behavior recurs, tell the student you will call the parent or guardian, and do so that same day. Tell the parent exactly why you are calling, and secure his or her support in helping the student control the behavior.

In the unlikely event that the behavior recurs a third time, refer the student to the counselor. Be sure to let the counselor know what actions you have already taken.

In the even more unlikely event that the behavior recurs a fourth time, refer the student to the assistant principal. Let the assistant principal know the actions you have already taken and that the behavior is disrupting your class.

Detentions may be helpful. The most effective penalty Tomas Gomez used was after-school detentions, which he conducted. School board policy allowed detentions if the student was given a twenty-four-hour notice (so that transportation could be arranged). A detention that you manage will give you the opportunity to work one on one with the recalcitrant student, or, if you have several, to work with them in a small group.

Tomas found that the detention time served as a catalyst to effective communication with students, and in many cases, students began to come after school of their own volition in order to get the attention they so desperately needed. Yes, this does add to your teaching day. Is it worth it? Yes.

If you teach in a school that you choose not to stay in after school is dismissed, you may want to consider before-school or lunchtime detentions. Tomas has also used lunchtime detentions with success. He did not keep detentions every day at lunch, however, because of the short lunch period. He kept detentions only on

Tuesdays and Thursdays, so that he had the other days free of obligations at lunchtime.

If the misbehavior is major and/or violent: Remove the student from the class. (Be sure to let the assistant principal or principal know exactly why the student is being removed.)

Then speak to the student.

Then speak to his or her parents or guardian.

Your message must be this: "I care for you as a person and as a student. I want you to be in my class. I want to help you learn, to gain control of your life, to be a successful person. You are a valuable human being. But that behavior (and the student needs to know exactly what behavior you're referring to) is unacceptable. I cannot allow it because it destroys what I am trying to create for you and for other students—a place where we are safe to learn and grow and become what we can be. So, the behavior must go. When it's gone, I want you back."

The student may be out for only a portion of one period, or, if administrators put him or her on indoor or outdoor suspension, the time may be longer.

When the student returns, reinforce the message that you want him or her in your class. If the tendency to violent behavior is consistent, as well it might be, you may want to agree on a signal to alert each other to the likelihood of flare-ups so that they can be averted.

IN CLOSING

To summarize, you must be consistent in managing your classroom. Your messages must be explicit, and they must be the same, day after day after day. These are the behaviors and attitudes expected in this classroom: enumerate them. These behaviors and attitudes are not acceptable in this classroom: enumerate them. The messages must be spoken, enacted, and pervasive.

When you get the behaviors and attitudes you want, praise them, specifically and generously, to students, parents, counselors, coaches, sponsors, administrators, and the community at large!

When you get something else, act—quickly and appropriately: first, by gently redirecting; if that doesn't work, by speaking directly to the student, apart from his or her peers; if that doesn't work, by speaking to parents or guardians; if that doesn't work, by referring the student to the counselor; and if that doesn't work, by referring the student to the assistant principal. The last resort is removing the student from the class—and from the opportunity to learn.

You must remember, too, that managing the classroom is your responsibility. While you may need occasional support from counselors and administrators, that support should be tapped only when essential and always with prior agreement. Members of the support staff are there to help in establishing a network of support for students, but they cannot and should not be held responsible for everything that goes on in your classroom.

RESOURCES

The best resources you will find for help in managing your classroom are next door, down the hall, around the corner, or in a neighboring school. They are your fellow teachers who have mastered the four steps described above. They will not be hard to find; just ask around about who the best teachers in your school or community are; they will be well known by students, parents, administrators, and other teachers.

Once you have found them, introduce yourself and open a conversation about teaching and learning. You will find many who will be happy to share what they know. Listen to what they say, take notes, try what they suggest, and go back for more conversation. When you find colleagues whose philosophy and approach agree with your own, arrange for peer observations. You should observe other teachers, and you should invite those whose counsel you especially value to observe you. And don't forget to pass the torch: when other teachers ask you for help, be generous in giving it.

You will find additional resources in professional literature, both printed and online. One that is especially good is Thomas R. McDaniel's "A Primer on Classroom Discipline: Principles Old and New," *Phi Delta Kappan* 68, no. 1 (September 1986). Available from the PDK Archives online (www.pdkintl.org), this is one of the best treatments of classroom management ever, and it is as pertinent now as it was when it was published.

PDK describes it: "McDaniel provides 10 principles, combining modern and traditional approaches, that can serve as guidelines for teachers on maintaining classroom discipline. These principles include focusing the student's attention on the teacher before beginning to teach, getting students on-task quickly and keeping them on-task consistently by monitoring them, using a soft, low-pitched voice, using nonverbal cues, controlling the classroom environment, and giving positive reinforcement. McDaniel includes a checklist on discipline for classroom teachers with which one can analyze classroom disciplinary practices."

Another useful resource is Bryan Goodwin's fine book, *Simply Better: Doing What Matters Most to Change the Odds for Student Success* (ASCD, 2011). Chapter 4, "Creating High-Performance School Cultures," discusses what it takes to establish a culture of high expectations for academics and behavior, not only in the individual classroom but also throughout the school.

William Glasser's ideas about the five basic needs—survival, belonging, fun, freedom, and power—form the foundation for Suzanne G. Houff's comprehensive book, *Managing the Classroom Environment: Meeting the Needs of the Student, 2nd Edition* (Rowman & Littlefield, 2013). Ms. Houff offers scenarios for analysis and emphasizes student responsibility and prevention first, intervention second.

Belinda Christine Tetteris, an elementary school teacher, shares practical ideas, visuals, and reproducible pages in her delightful book, *The Nitty-Gritty Classroom and Behavior Management Resource: Strategies, Reproducibles, and Tips for Teachers* (Rowman & Littlefield, 2006). She includes a section on differentiating lessons according to student needs.

In *Resistant Students: Reach Me Before You Teach Me* (Rowman & Littlefield, 2012), Mary Skvorak elaborates on the premise that successful classroom management rests on a relationship of trust between teacher and student. As one reviewer points out, "Her examples of dialogue between teacher and student reflect deep understanding of the relationships that are possible when we rest our own agendas and begin to listen to what our students need from us as people before they can learn from us as teachers."

Carol S. Dweck's book, *Mindset: The New Psychology of Success, How We Can Learn to Fulfill Our Potential* (Ballantine Books, 2008), mentioned in the preface, is a must-have resource for teachers, not only to help with classroom management but also to illuminate the nature of our development as human beings.

NOTES

1. This and the following exercise are modeled after some in Richard Curwin and Barbara Fuhrmann's *Discovering Your Teaching Self* (New York: Prentice Hall, 1975).

2. For a compelling discussion of this issue, see Po Bronson and Ashley Merryman's *NurtureShock* (New York: Hatchette Book Group, 2009). The first chapter, "The Inverse Power of Praise," should be required reading for both parents and teachers.

Chapter Three

Differentiated Instruction

Effective instruction requires a teacher to accommodate a myriad of learning styles, interests, interferences, and abilities while at the same time maintaining high expectations and paving the way for every student's success. Knowing how to do that is the subject of this section. What follows is based on three assumptions:

1. What teachers want for each student is maximum development during the time that child is in their care.
2. While the desirable knowledge and skills for a given grade level or course may be the same for all children, the speed and means by which those results are attained will differ from student to student.
3. If teachers believe the first two assumptions, they must embrace the idea that all of their students do not have to be doing the same thing at the same time.

When teachers act on those assumptions, they differentiate instruction. By the time you finish reading this section, the term will hold no mystery for you. Many teachers who read this will say to themselves, "Well, I'm already doing that! I didn't know that was differentiating instruction!" Others may think, "Is that all there is to it? I can do that!" Some may think, "That sounds like a lot of hard work." For accomplished teachers who already differentiate instruction, what follows may add some new wrinkles to your repertoire; for the novice, it may prove to hasten the refinement of your craft.

If it turns out that differentiating instruction is a new approach for your teaching, the persistence and patience it deserves will yield huge payoffs in terms of student learning. Start small, build on your successes, learn from your failures, and don't quit—because this is the *only* way you can help all of your students gain maximum growth.

Teaching is much like old-fashioned country dances. The men and boys lined up on one side of the dance floor, the women and girls on the other. When the music started, the gentlemen walked across the floor, chose partners, and then led the dance for the three or four minutes the song lasted. When the music stopped, they escorted the ladies back to their places.

Teaching is like that. Teachers have their classes for a brief dance only—usually 180 days—and secondary teachers may see their students only an hour or two a day. In that short time, they must dance well, for they may have only that one opportunity to touch the lives of their students. They need to know the difference they want to make and have the means at their disposal to make it. Differentiated instruction is one of those means, a basic step every teacher needs to know.

DIFFERENTIATED INSTRUCTION: WHAT IT IS

Differentiated instruction is teaching that accommodates most of the learning needs of all of the children in a class, enabling each child to attain the desired academic results. It is therefore teaching that is based on the teacher's clear understanding of each child's talents, interests, learning styles, and learning interferences, if any.

Differentiated instruction is not the same in every classroom, nor is it the same from one year to the next for a given teacher. It is the unique blend of each teacher's responses to the needs of current students. Those responses are determined by ongoing assessment of students' progress combined with artful adjustment of opportunities for learning. The differentiated classroom is therefore characterized by a continuous loop of assessment and instruction, by learning groups that change with students' needs and interests, by a rich variety of resources, and by intense, purposeful activity.

Differentiated instruction may be as simple as providing accommodations for special physical needs, such as seating a child close to the front of a reading circle in order for the teacher to be seen and heard easily, and it may be as complex as the rare instance of providing an individualized course of study for each student in the class.

Most often, it falls somewhere in between, with the teacher offering instruction to the whole class and then providing follow-up activities or assignments that allow students the opportunity to build on what they already know and to learn what they need to know, in different ways and at different speeds. Examples of these "degrees of differentiation" will be given in some detail in the "What It Looks Like" and the "How to Do It" sections that follow.

Using differentiated instruction wisely is like feeding a large family. The aim is the same for all: maximum nourishment for health and growth. The basic diet is also the same for all: whole grains, fresh fruit, plenty of vegetables, protein, and fiber. However, the nutritional needs for the toddler are far different from those of the teen, and the needs for the children differ from those of the adults.

That reality is acknowledged every day in healthy homes. You don't prepare a completely different menu for every person in the family, but you do offer choices and portion sizes that accommodate their individual needs. Should one member of the family require a special diet, that diet is prepared along with the food for the rest of the family, and when meals are served, everyone is well—and appropriately—fed.

In classrooms where differentiated instruction is most successful, the teacher and the students share the work of teaching and learning. Norma Bossard, a master teacher who left a legacy of love and learning, used to tell her children at the beginning of the school year that they were about to take a journey together. For example, when she was teaching third grade, she would tell the children to imagine that they were all leaving the Second Grade Shore in a boat that would take them across the Third Grade River; at the end of the year, they would all arrive on the Fourth Grade Shore.

Then she emphasized the word *all* and told the children that keeping everyone "in the boat" was everyone's responsibility, not just hers. She reported that periodically, one child or another would come to her and say something like, "Ms. Bossard, I think Danny is falling out of the boat!" That was Norma's cue to say, "Well, what do you think we should do about it?" Then they would plan a strategy to get the wayward child back on track. Her boat story helped everyone in her classroom share the responsibility for success.

Any teacher who attempts to differentiate instruction will find, as Norma did, that students' "ownership" of their learning is a key ingredient in the process. That "ownership" will contribute immeasurably to the ambiance of the classroom and to the speed with which students achieve desired results.

TO WHAT EXTENT DO YOU ALREADY DIFFERENTIATE INSTRUCTION?

Use this checklist to assess the extent to which you already differentiate instruction.

No.	Descriptive Statement	Put an X Beneath the Most Appropriate Response			
		Never	Rarely	Occasionally	Frequently
1.	Measurable objectives for what students need to learn are communicated to students, parents, and guardians.				
2.	Before instruction begins, assessments are used to determine what students already know and what they need to know.				
3.	The activities that students pursue in class are clearly linked both to the desired results and to students' needs and talents.				
4.	Students have some choice in their classroom activities.				
5.	The assignments that students complete out of class are clearly linked both to the desired results and to students' needs and talents.				
6.	Students have some choice in their out-of-class assignments.				
7.	Assessment (by both student and teacher) that uses clear criteria is an integral part of the learning process.				
8.	Various kinds of assessment are employed (e.g., portfolios, projects, oral reports, PowerPoint presentations, demonstrations, pencil-and-paper tests, skits).				
9.	Assessment results are used to plan further learning.				

10. Whole-group instruction regularly requires students to speak, listen, read, write, see, and move.

11. Students work in small groups based on needs, interests, and preferences.

12. Group composition changes as students' needs dictate.

13. A management system that affords easy access to information concerning each student's progress is employed.

14. Assignments and activities help all students to develop study skills, research skills, and higher-level thinking skills.

15. Students plan and monitor their own learning and know how to change the plan when necessary.

16. Each student's progress is regularly made clear to the student and to the parents or guardians.

17. When a student needs more than I can provide in order to learn effectively, I recommend specialists (e.g., tutors, speech therapists) or testing.

Instructions: Scan the completed checklist to see where most of your checkmarks are located. If you have more on the left-hand side (for never or rarely), you may want to consider restructuring your teaching in order to address individual needs more effectively. The rest of this book should be helpful. If most of your checkmarks are on the right-hand side (for occasionally or frequently), you are clearly attending to the individual needs of your students. The rest of this book will endorse what you are doing and perhaps give you some additional ideas.

WHAT IT LOOKS LIKE

In Elementary School

Mid-semester in Donna Victor's first-grade classroom, three children were huddled around a science experiment, several more were helping themselves to books from a well-stocked reading corner, one child was working on a geography program at the computer, some were illustrating their own stories, and still others were gathered for a guided reading lesson with the teacher.

Donna sat so that she could see all of the students while focusing primarily on those with whom she was working. When the guided reading lesson was completed, Donna scanned the room to be sure other children were ready to change activities. The children at the science table needed a few more minutes to finish, so Donna extended the conversation with her group about the story they had read, and everyone stayed put until the experiment was finished.

Then the children rotated stations, so that Donna could work with those who had been in the reading corner; the children at the science table moved to the reading corner, the children who had illustrated their stories moved to the science table, and the children who left the teacher began illustrating their stories. Because the child working at the computer required more time than most to finish his work, he remained where he was.

In about one hour, the four groups had rotated to all four stations, or centers, and the child at the computer had worked thirty minutes on the geography lesson, joined one group for the science experiment, and participated in the guided reading lesson with others on his reading level. Donna later discussed the accommodations for that child's independent reading and illustration of his story; she said that she was in close touch with his mother, who would supervise those two activities at home.

This use of centers, or stations, is an effective means of differentiating instruction in elementary school. In the primary grades (kindergarten, grades 1 and 2), the teacher can give instructions for all of the centers before children separate into their groups, and then the teacher's role is to monitor the time and to work with whichever group needs attention. In the intermediate grades (grades 3 through 5), written instructions can be provided at each center for children to read and follow.

What children do at the centers is determined by their instructional needs and/or their interests. In the example given above, children were grouped by their reading levels, and the four guided reading lessons were on four different levels. In this instance, the science experiment was the same for all of the children; the reading corner included books on all of the children's reading levels, and the illustration of original stories was totally individualized.

Sarah Jones, a teacher of children with varying exceptionalities, demonstrated one of the most remarkable instances of accommodating a child's needs. On a typical day, Sarah moved among her students, helping each with the task at hand. She was accompanied throughout by a little girl who clung to her teacher's shirttail, following every step of the way.

Sarah explained later that the child who followed her so closely was not yet secure enough to stay in her own seat. In order to accommodate the little girl without literally holding her hand all day, Sarah always wore a shirt or blouse that the child could hold on to. Most teachers will not encounter an emotional need so demanding; may those who do have the same patience and compassion demonstrated by Sarah.

In Middle School

James McReady teaches Algebra I to eighth-graders for high school credit in an urban middle school. At the beginning of each term, James allows his students to choose their partners (two or three). The self-selected triads or quartets stay together as long as all of the students in them make gains; if anyone shows unsatisfactory progress, James rearranges the groups.

Combined with direct whole-group instruction that gives plenty of examples with unconditional support for all of his students (many of whom speak no English), this informal cooperative learning comprises the major approach for James's classes. Students work with their partners to solve problems after each whole-group lesson; they do their homework together, either on campus after school or by telephone, email, or texting from home in the evenings; and they study for tests together.

James makes himself available during class, during part of the lunch period two days a week, and before and after school. He reported that it is rare for an individual student to seek him out. "They rely on their partners more than they rely on me," James says. True interdependence—it is one of the two factors essential for success in cooperative learning. The other factor, independent accountability, is built into periodic tests.

Each student must take tests without help from partners; the test scores are James's measures of individual progress. According to school administrators, James's approach has yielded uncommon success; nearly all of his students earn As or Bs, high school credit, and the opportunity to accelerate their study of mathematics when they reach ninth grade.

Carrie London was confronted with a different kind of challenge in her seventh-grade language arts class. Among her students was Ronnie Walton, an energetic motorcycle enthusiast who had not yet learned to read. After trying several approaches to engage him in activities with other students, all of which resulted in his disrupting the class, Carrie gave up on conventional avenues and bought a stack of motorcycle magazines. She let Ronnie look at the magazines every day in class, and, to her delight, he began to ask for help in deciphering the text.

When Carrie realized that she couldn't teach the rest of the students and also answer all of Ronnie's questions, she moved him next to Anna, who was able to maintain her A and help Ronnie as well. By the end of the school year, Ronnie still had gaps in his learning, but he was reading well enough to move into an eighth-grade class and do grade-level work.

In High School

When Paul Mora taught Expository Writing to tenth-graders, his students, with approval from their parents, signed "contracts" for their work. They could elect a contract that would result in a final grade of C, representing adequate grade-level performance; B, representing good work; or A, representing excellence. They could not choose to do D or F work.

Basic conditions of each contract were the same: students had to do the assigned work to the best of their ability and turn it in on time. If, on any assignment, they earned less than the grade for which they had contracted, they could revise the assignment for a higher grade. The descriptions in the contracts included all of the assignments and the dates they were due. Assignments were of three types: compositions, grammar and usage exercises, and vocabulary lessons. Both the quantity and the complexity of the assignments differed in the three contracts.

The class was organized for a combination of whole-group, small-group, and individualized instruction, and each kind of instruction was scheduled at the same time every week. This pattern established a routine with which the students and teacher were comfortable, and all knew what to expect each day of school.

On Mondays and Wednesdays, the first half of the period was devoted to whole-group instruction: Paul taught the basic concepts necessary for writing effective exposition, modeled rhetorical strategies that the students could use in their compositions, and shared examples that demonstrated the concepts or skills under study. The second half of the class was devoted to practicing whatever had been demonstrated in the lesson.

Tuesdays and Thursdays were "lab days," when students brought their work to class and worked individually. If they needed help from Paul, they took a number from the holder on the desk (their "deli numbers," suggested by a student). Paul called the numbers in sequence and worked with students one at a time to help them solve their writing problems. Students were free to call on each other if peers could answer their questions. If a student was in need of Paul's help on a composition and was holding a number somewhere "down the line," the composition could be put aside and the grammar or vocabulary work pursued until Paul called the number that would bring the student to his desk.

Fridays were reserved for sharing and skill building. As Paul assessed compositions, he highlighted portions or identified whole papers that deserved to be read aloud to the class; that reading was done on Fridays. As he identified students who had difficulty with particular skills (such as subject-verb agreement or punctuation rules), he planned mini-lessons to address those skills with small groups of students; those mini-lessons were also delivered on Fridays. Students whose work had not revealed the need for the mini-lesson could listen to it if they chose or work on their own assignments.

This approach to differentiating instruction was a welcome change for both students and teacher. All of the students passed the class, and few of them failed to earn the grade they wanted. They appreciated having a choice about the quantity and difficulty of assignments, and Paul appreciated not having to badger them about assignments that they didn't want to do. According to Paul, the increased record keeping was a small price to pay for the success of the venture.

Simon Grainger, a biology teacher in the same school, devised a successful means of accommodating a challenging student in his class. Teddy Palmer was well known throughout the school; his mental gymnastics included always knowing what time it was on the moon and other esoteric facts, which he volubly shared with anyone who would listen. His social skills were delayed, so dealing with him effectively took a great deal of patience.

Knowing that classmates would be taxed by Teddy's presence in the small groups required for lab work, Simon sent Teddy on an errand to the office one day early in the term and then told the rest of the class that their way of helping Teddy through biology would be to share the responsibility: on each lab day Simon would assign Teddy to a different group—and that group's performance would be assessed not only on the basis of how well they completed the lab but also on how well they helped Teddy. This "classroom conspiracy" resulted in a cohesive and supportive network for including a child who might otherwise have been an outcast.

BEFORE YOU START

Two things before you begin: First, differentiated instruction works in all kinds of schools. Donna Victor's, Sarah Jones's, and James McReady's schools are all overcrowded schools in poor urban neighborhoods. Carrie London's middle school is in a working-class neighborhood of a large city, and the high school mentioned was serving a middle- to upper-middle-class community when Paul Mora and Simon Grainger taught there. Successful differentiated instruction is practiced in public, private, and parochial school, with both large and small classes, and with heterogeneous as well as homogeneous groups.

Second, differentiated instruction requires a well-managed classroom. It is successful in classes that are orderly and well organized. Because its success frequently depends upon the use of small groups, students need to know how to work together without disturbing others. Differentiated instruction will contribute to good behavior because of the purposeful, student-centered work it requires, but respectful behavior is a necessary prerequisite for its launching.

HOW TO DO IT

Reading the descriptions of what differentiated instruction looks like in practice should have given you some pretty good ideas about how to do it. As the vignettes suggest, no one way is always the best way; your approach will depend on the needs of your students. On the other hand, consistently following some general guidelines in your teaching cycle will lay the foundation for differentiating instruction, making it easier for you to accommodate individual differences.

The Teaching Cycle

Like all effective teaching, differentiated instruction begins when the teacher starts thinking about the approaching school year, and it ends when the teacher reflects on the year just past. The steps in the cycle of teaching between those two points are described below.

1. *Know what you are aiming for.* The grade level or course targets must be absolutely clear to you. You must know what your students need to know and be able to do when they leave you at the end of the term. The results may be specified for you in a state, district, or school curriculum, or they may be open to your judgment. Either way, before you ever begin, you need to know your destination.

2. Find or create one or more assessments that will tell you each student's starting point. Keeping the destination in mind, assess what your students know at the outset. You will no doubt find that some of them have already mastered some of the knowledge and skills required by your curriculum; others may need to learn it all.

The assessment may be as simple as an observational checklist, or it may be as complex as a battery of diagnostic instruments that address various skills and concepts in your grade level or course. The assessment should be relatively easy to score, and the results should be easy for you to interpret. Whatever you create or select should yield data that will be useful to you in planning what and how to teach.

3. Collect additional information about your students that will help you in planning. Look at the school's records. Do some of your children have documented learning disabilities and Individual Education Plans (IEPs) that you need to follow? Also, ask your students how they learn most effectively. If they don't know, your questions (or additional assessments) may help them—and you—find out. Observe your students closely to add to your knowledge of their habits and attitudes. Talk to their parents or guardians early in the year. Find out everything you can that will help you help them.

4. Divide the year's (or term's) work into segments: thematic units of study, logical blocks of skills, or some other logical "chunks" of the course or grade content. If you are responsible for grade-level instruction or for teaching several subjects at once, keep in mind that interdisciplinary thematic units will enable you to integrate instruction effectively. If you teach a skills-based subject, the content may dictate another approach. This step should result in a timeline that covers the entire year, with major topics or themes and the number of weeks devoted to each.

5. *Plan the first unit or block of instruction.* Decide:

- What knowledge and/or skills must be mastered during the unit
- How the knowledge and skills might be demonstrated and assessed
- What activities students could participate in that will lead to mastery

As you plan, think about options. For example, students can learn content by listening to lectures, viewing films, searching the library or the Internet, reading books, interviewing experts, or watching demonstrations. They can demonstrate knowledge and skills by writing reports, giving oral recitations, creating dioramas, making posters, producing a play, creating a product, or compiling a portfolio.

As you list options suitable for this unit of study, be sure to keep in mind what you learned about your students from the initial assessment and from your investigation of individual learning needs.

This is the point at which you plan enrichment for students who have already mastered the basic knowledge and skills to be covered in this unit—not more of what they already know (more problems, longer assignments, etc.), but new, more complex, more challenging work, work that will keep them engaged and excited about learning. It is also the point at which you plan accommodations for children with special learning needs, including those who may be starting the year with a deficit in background knowledge or fundamental skills. For these children, the work must be carefully sequenced, leading to the eventual results that you intend for all students. It cannot be simply a "watered down" version of core content.

Decide which aspects of the instruction (if any) you must teach directly in order to ensure all students' knowledge of content and mastery of skills. For example, Donna Victor needed to teach the reading lesson, James McReady needed to control all of the content in his algebra class, and Paul Mora needed to teach the rhetorical strategies required for effective exposition. Teachers who are proficient in differentiated instruction retain control over few aspects of instruction, preferring student-centered, inquiry-based approaches for as much of the content as possible.

Some of the content you keep within your control will undoubtedly be taught to the whole class. As you plan for whole-group instruction, keep the following guidelines in mind and you will cover most of the bases in terms of learning styles, preferences, and individual needs:

In every lesson:

- Students should speak, not only to the teacher but also to each other. (That suggests cooperative learning groups, or, at the least, learning with partners.)
- They should listen, not only to the teacher but also to each other.
- They should read something every day (and if they use Reciprocal Teaching, the SQ3R [Survey, Question, Read, Recite, Review], or Directed Reading-Thinking Activities, so much the better).
- They should write, both to learn and to report what they know.
- They should move. Adults don't do well when they have to sit for longer than forty-five minutes; why should they expect students to?
- They should see; at least part of every lesson should be illustrated with visual cues.

Decide which aspects of instruction students may pursue through other means. Donna Victor knew that her first-graders could handle the science experiment, select their own books for independent reading, and illustrate their stories without help. She also knew that one child required additional time at the computer.

Although James McReady taught all of the concepts and skills in his algebra class, he allowed his students freedom to choose their partners and to practice the skills in small groups. Paul Mora knew that his tenth-graders could complete their compositions, grammar exercises, and vocabulary assignments with help tailored to individual needs.

Insofar as possible, plan for your students to choose both their means of learning content and their methods of demonstrating knowledge. Their options for choices will be influenced by your knowledge of their needs, talents, and interests.

6. *Proceed according to plan.* Conduct the unit, offering direct instruction when desirable, monitoring students' work, coaching individuals, accommodating special needs, and continually assessing each child's progress. Help your students to keep track of their own learning. Wang, Haertel, and Walberg's important research reported that the foremost factor in students' learning is the "student's capacity to plan, monitor, and if necessary, re-plan learning strategies."[1]

7. *At the end of the unit, evaluate each student's progress, and evaluate the unit itself.* Regarding student progress: Which students attained all of the objectives? Which ones need additional help on some of the knowledge or skills? Regarding the unit: What went well? What needed refinement? What will you change for next year? Keep good records; they will serve you well. If you maintain a reflective log, as recommended in the first section of this book, the log is the logical place for these notes.

8. *Repeat the process with the remaining segments of content.* Using your most recent assessment as a guide, plan the next unit. Build in the necessary reteaching of essential skills taught in the previous unit. By the end of the year or term, all of your students, including those with learning disabilities, should have mastered the necessary knowledge and skills. Some of them will have exceeded expectations.

Note: Keep parents informed of their children's progress throughout the year, and solicit their support in helping children learn.

IF YOU'RE APPREHENSIVE

Remember the advice given earlier: Start small, build on your successes, learn from your failures, and don't quit.

Also, see "Making the Case for Differentiation" (Birnie, 2015), which examines the faulty thinking behind three frequent arguments against differentiation: it's just another fad, it requires a separate lesson plan for each student, and it isn't worth the time.

As you overcome anxiety, gain confidence, and build on your successes, you'll find that your students are learning more than ever—and enjoying the process.

RESOURCES

If the ideas here whet your appetite for a larger meal, many authoritative resources are available. Several are named below. In addition, a bounty of resources exists on the Internet; just use the key words *differentiated instruction,* and go from there. Or start with the website for the Association of Supervision and Curriculum Development (www.ascd.org); look especially for the 1999 ASCD book *The Differentiated Classroom: Responding to the Needs of All Learners* by Carol Ann Tomlinson. (Figure 2.1, Differentiation of Instruction, is worth the price of the book.)

Other terms that will lead you to research and practice in the art of differentiated instruction are these: *learning styles, teaching styles, multiple intelligences, brain-based research, authentic assessment, rubrics, graphic organizers, direct instruction, cooperative learning, information processing, inquiry-based learning.*

To gain an understanding of early thinking on differentiation, read *A School for Everyone: Design for a Middle, Junior, or Senior*

High School That Combines the Old and the New (National Association of Secondary School Principals, 1977) by J. Lloyd Trump. Considered by many to be "the father of differentiated instruction" and one of the greatest educational leaders of the twentieth century, Dr. Trump made significant contributions to innovations in school organization, differentiated staffing, team teaching, and flexible scheduling as well as differentiated instruction.

Margaret Beecher's *Developing the Gifts and Talents of All Students in the Regular Classroom* (Creative Learning Press, 1996) is a wonderful book, with an introduction that offers frameworks and models for differentiating curriculum, including the "Principles of Differentiating Curriculum for the Gifted and Talented." Those principles are invaluable to teachers who work with talented children. Beyond the introduction, the book tells how to use "The Enrichment Triad" in the regular classroom, giving modifications for primary, elementary, and middle school classrooms.

Sue Bredekamp and Carol Copple edited *Developmentally Appropriate Practice in Early Childhood Programs* (National Association for the Education of Young Children, 2002), which should be required reading for anyone who teaches in the primary grades. Particularly related to the subject of differentiated instruction are the sections on "Using Knowledge of Individual Children to Inform Practice" and "Responding to Individual and Cultural Variation."

Teachers of grades 5 through 12 will appreciate *Differentiated Instruction: Content Area Applications and Other Considerations for Teaching in Grades 5–12 in the Twenty-First Century* (Rowman & Littlefield, 2013), a comprehensive collection of ideas edited by Ervin Sparapani. This book covers nearly every aspect of the subject, from using technology to differentiating instruction for students with severe disabilities. As one of the book's reviewers said, "Ervin Sparapani presents a new look at differentiated instruction, tackling issues previously ignored by other authors. The inclusion of curriculum experts, differentiation for higher-order thinking, and technology's role in differentiation sets this book apart from others of its types."

Those who teach at-risk students will benefit from Rita Dunn and Andrea Honigsfeld's *Differentiating Instruction for At-Risk Students: What to Do and How to Do It* (Rowman & Littlefield, 2009). Drawing on their extensive knowledge of learning styles, the authors focus on approaches that best reach at-risk students. Their applications cover literacy, mathematics, science, and social studies in both elementary and secondary schools.

Gayle Gregory and Carolyn Chapman's book *Differentiated Instructional Strategies: One Size Doesn't Fit All* (Corwin Press, 2002) is another valuable resource that has guided scores of teachers in their efforts to differentiate instruction. The tone of the book is especially engaging; in their acknowledgments, the authors dedicate the book "to children everywhere in the hope that its content will help teachers meet their needs and empower learners to reach their potential and be the best they can be with joy, enthusiasm, creativity, and self-confidence."

Additional resources are no doubt down the hall, around the corner, across the street, in the form of colleagues who are successfully practicing the techniques described. You should plan to feast on both the printed materials and the examples from other teachers.

A WORD ABOUT HIGH-STAKES TESTING

Many teachers live and work in environments that are suffused with anxiety about high-stakes testing. They fear to do anything in the classroom other than prepare students for the tests. Their fear is too often fueled, and in some cases generated, by principals and district leaders who themselves are under pressure to improve student performance. Such fear paralyzes teachers and condemns students to an unpalatable diet of worksheets that mimic test questions. Such a diet inevitably leads to intellectual malnourishment.

Instead of producing better students and higher test scores, it diminishes students' desire to learn and teachers' desire to teach. Ultimately, it sabotages any prospect of genuine student success.

High-stakes tests are here to stay. They are the yardsticks by which children's academic performance is gauged and by which the quality of our schools is measured. They are useful measures for those purposes. And they should certainly be considered when professionals identify academic standards in order to develop curriculum. However, no one ever intended for those tests (or facsimiles of them) to *become* the curriculum. High-stakes tests should be taken in stride and recognized for what they are: just one measure of progress in children's educational journey.

The research on high-performing schools reports that children do well when the academic goals are clear, when tests are used frequently to measure progress, and when instruction addresses gaps in learning revealed by the tests. Basic skills of listening, speaking, reading, and writing are taught in carefully sequenced lessons. Curriculum is rich, instructional strategies engage students in their work, and hard work is rewarded. Such research supports the use of differentiated instruction as a primary approach to teaching. It also recognizes that high-performing schools are places where teachers and children both want to be; they are places where school days are greeted, not with fear, but with joy.

NOTE

1. Margaret C. Wang, Geneva D. Haertel, and Herbert J. Walberg, "What Helps Students Learn?" *Educational Leadership*, December 1993/January 1994:74–79.

References

Beecher, Margaret. 1996. *Developing the Gifts and Talents of All Students in the Regular Classroom*. Mansfield Center, CT: Creative Learning Press.

Birnie, Billie F. 2015. Making the Case for Differentiation. *The Clearing House: A Journal of Educational Strategies, Issues and Ideas*, 88:2, 62–65.

Birnie, Billie F. 2016. Promoting Civil Discourse in the Classroom. *Kappa Delta Pi Record*, 52:2, 52–55.

Bredekamp, Sue, and Copple, Carol, Editors. 2002. *Developmentally Appropriate Practice in Early Childhood Programs*, Revised edition. Washington, DC: National Association for the Education of Young Children.

Bronson, Po, and Merryman, Ashley. 2009. *NurtureShock*. New York: Hatchette Book Group.

Curwin, Richard, and Fuhrmann, Barbara. 1975. *Discovering Your Teaching Self*. New Jersey: Prentice-Hall.

Dunn, Rita, and Honigsfeld, Andrea. 2009. *Differentiating Instruction for At-Risk Students: What to Do and How to Do It*. Lanham, MD: Rowman & Littlefield.

Dweck, Carol S. 2008. *Mindset: The New Psychology of Success, How We Can Learn to Fulfill Our Potential*. New York: Ballantine Books.

Goodwin, Bryan. 2011. *Simply Better: Doing What Matters Most to Change the Odds for Student Success*. Alexandria, VA: Association for Supervision and Curriculum Development.

Gregory, Gayle H., and Chapman, Carolyn. 2002. *Differentiated Instructional Strategies: One Size Doesn't Fit All*. Thousand Oaks, CA: Corwin Press.

Houff, Suzanne G. 2013. *Managing the Classroom Environment: Meeting the Needs of the Student, 2nd Edition*. Lanham, MD: Rowman & Littlefield.

Jarson, Jennifer. 2015. Dear Diary: Using a Reflective Teaching Journal for Improvement and Assessment? (Blog).http://acrlog.org/2015/09/04/dear-diary-using-a-reflective-teaching-journal-for-improvement-and-assessment/.

McDaniel, Thomas R. 1986. A Primer on Classroom Discipline: Principles Old and New. *Phi Delta Kappan*, 68:1.

Sellers, Paul. 2016. Journalling for Woodworkers. (Blog).https://paulsellers.com/2016/06/journalling-for-woodworkers/.

Skvorak, Mary. 2012. *Resistant Students: Reach Me Before You Teach Me*. Lanham, MD: Rowman & Littlefield.

Sparapani, Ervin F. 2013. *Differentiated Instruction: Content Area Applications and Other Considerations for Teaching in Grades 5–12 in the Twenty-First Century*. Lanham, MD: Rowman & Littlefield.

Tetteris, Belinda Christine. 2006. *The Nitty-Gritty Classroom and Behavior Management Resource: Strategies, Reproducibles, and Tips for Teachers*. Lanham, MD: Rowman & Littlefield.

Tomlinson, Carol Ann. 1999. *The Differentiated Classroom: Responding to the Needs of All Learners*. Alexandria, VA: Association for Supervision and Curriculum Development.

Trump, J. Lloyd. 1977. *A School for Everyone: Design for a Middle, Junior, or Senior High School That Combines the Old and the New*. Reston, VA: National Association of Secondary School Principals.

Wang, Margaret C., Haertel, Geneva D., and Walberg, Herbert J. 1994. What Helps Students Learn? *Educational Leadership*, December 1993/January 1994:74–79.

About the Author

Billie F. Birnie has been teaching most of her life, first to students in elementary, middle, and senior high schools, and in recent years, to prospective and experienced teachers. Her published writing ranges from poetry and memoir to professional articles and books on teaching and learning. Dr. Birnie has received numerous awards for her work in education: she was named Teacher of the Year in two large urban high schools, Distinguished Alumnus by the University of Miami School of Education, and Educator of the Year by Florida International University. She can be contacted at bfbirnie@icloud.com.

CPSIA information can be obtained
at www.ICGtesting.com
Printed in the USA
BVOW08s2030280217
477410BV00001B/2/P